BRUSSELS TRAVEL GUIDE 2023

Your Essential Handbook for Budget Travelers, Packed with Insider Tips, Seasonal Delights, Free Adventures, Safety Savvy, and More

TABLE OF CONTENTS

INTRODUCTION

Welcome to Brussels, the land of chocolate, waffles, and all things amazing! I'm so stoked that you're here because let me tell you, this city is like a treasure trove waiting to be discovered. Prepare to have the best time of your life!
What's the big deal? Let me explain it to you, my friend.

Picture this: cobblestone streets winding through centuries-old architecture, mouthwatering smells wafting from cozy cafes, and a vibrant atmosphere that just screams "good times ahead." Yep, that's Brussels in a nutshell.

But wait, there's more! Brussels isn't your typical run-of-the-mill city. It's like a funky mixtape, blending history, culture, and a whole lot of quirkiness. Seriously, where else can you find a tiny peeing statue called Manneken Pis stealing the spotlight? Legends are formed of this stuff!

Now, I know what you might be thinking: "Brussels must be crazy expensive, right?" Well, hold onto your socks because I'm about to drop a truth bomb on you. Brussels can be budget-friendly! Yes, you heard me right. With a little know-how and a dash of insider tips, you can experience the best of this city without watching your wallet cry tears of despair.

That's why we've put together this awesome guide for you. We've done the research, pounded the pavement, and hunted down the best deals, so you don't have to. My friend, we have your back!

Together, we'll dive into the heart of Brussels, uncovering hidden gems, exploring charming neighborhoods, and indulging in delicious treats that will make your taste buds dance with joy. We'll show you how to navigate public transportation like a pro, find affordable accommodations that won't make you break a sweat, and discover all the epic sights and sounds that make Brussels one of a kind.

So, my fellow adventurer, get ready for a wild ride through Brussels. We're here to make sure you have the time of your life without maxing out your credit card. It's gonna be educational, fun, and filled with memories that will last a lifetime. Are you ready? Let's do this, my friend! Brussels, here we come!

About This Guide

Hey there, curious traveler! Before we dive into the nitty-gritty of exploring Brussels on a budget, let me take a moment to tell you about this awesome guide that's gonna be your trusty sidekick on this adventure.

This guide is designed with one thing in mind: to help you make the most of your time in Brussels without burning a hole in your pocket. We know that traveling on a budget can sometimes feel like a puzzle, but fear not! We've got all the pieces right here, neatly organized and ready for you to put together.

Think of this guide as your personal treasure map, leading you to all the hidden gems, secret deals, and insider tips that will make your Brussels experience unforgettable. We've scoured the city, talked to locals, and put our backpacker hats on to bring you the most up-to-date information and recommendations.

But hey, this isn't your typical stuffy guidebook. No way! We've spiced things up with a casual, friendly tone that feels like you're chatting with a friend. We'll sprinkle in some stories, metaphors, and rhetorical questions to keep things interesting. After all, who wants to read a dry, boring guide when you're about to embark on an exciting adventure?

In each chapter, you'll find a wealth of knowledge that covers everything from getting to Brussels on a budget to finding the best cheap eats and affordable accommodations. We'll guide you through the must-see attractions, introduce you to the local culture, and even share some budget-friendly day trip options that will take your Brussels experience to the next level.

So, whether you're a broke student, a savvy backpacker, or simply someone who loves stretching their dollar to the max, this guide is for you. Get ready to unlock the secrets of Brussels on a budget and create memories that will last a lifetime.

Are you excited? I sure am! Let's jump right in and start this adventure together. Brussels is waiting, my friend, and we're about to show you the time of your life without breaking the bank. Let's go!

Brussels on a Budget

Ah, Brussels, a city of wonders that doesn't have to cost you an arm and a leg! If you're a budget-conscious traveler like me, get ready to explore this charming Belgian capital without breaking the bank. Brussels offers a wealth of affordable experiences, delightful culinary delights, and captivating sights that will make your wallet do a happy dance.

First things first, let's talk about accommodation. Brussels has a wide range of budget-friendly options, from cozy hostels to affordable guesthouses. By choosing strategically located accommodations and taking advantage of online deals and promotions, you can find a comfortable place to rest your weary head without draining your savings.

Now, let's move on to food. Oh boy, Brussels knows how to satisfy your taste buds without emptying your wallet. Street food is a must-try here, with mouthwatering frites and scrumptious waffles available at every corner. Local markets also offer fresh produce, delectable cheeses, and mouth watering chocolates at reasonable prices, allowing you to indulge in the flavors of Belgium without breaking the bank.

When it comes to sightseeing, Brussels has plenty to offer without a hefty price tag. Stroll through the iconic Grand Place, a UNESCO World Heritage site, marveling at the stunning architecture that surrounds you. Explore the vibrant neighborhoods of Marolles and Sablon, where you'll find charming streets, quirky boutiques, and lively flea markets.

Don't forget to take advantage of Brussels' excellent public transportation system, including buses and trams, which will whisk you around the city at a fraction of the cost of a taxi. And with the abundance of free museums, parks, and gardens, you'll have no shortage of budget-friendly activities to enjoy.

So, my fellow adventurer, get ready to immerse yourself in the magic of Brussels without breaking the bank. With some savvy planning, a sprinkle of insider tips, and a sense of adventure, you can create an unforgettable experience in this captivating city. Let's explore Brussels on a budget and make memories that will last a lifetime, all while keeping our wallets happy. Cheers to affordable adventures!

PLANNING YOUR BUDGET TRIP

When to Visit

Brussels, with its unique charm and vibrant atmosphere, welcomes visitors throughout the year. But let's talk about the best time to visit, shall we? Timing is key when it comes to experiencing the city at its finest while keeping your budget in check.

One of the most popular times to visit Brussels is during the spring (April to June) and early autumn (September to October). The weather is generally pleasant, with mild temperatures and a good amount of sunshine. During these months, you can enjoy exploring the city's outdoor attractions, strolling through parks, and savoring a leisurely drink at an outdoor café. Plus, the crowds tend to be slightly smaller compared to the peak summer season.

Speaking of summer (July and August), it's a time when Brussels comes alive with festivals, concerts, and cultural events. The city's squares transform into bustling hubs of activity, offering a lively atmosphere and an array of outdoor festivities. However, do keep in mind that this is the peak tourist season, so prices for accommodations and flights may be higher. If you're planning to visit during summer, consider booking well in advance to secure the best deals.

For those who prefer a more budget-friendly option, the winter months (November to February) offer a unique experience in Brussels. The city takes on a magical atmosphere, especially during the Christmas season, with charming Christmas markets, festive decorations, and ice-skating rinks popping up throughout the city. While the temperatures can be chilly, this is a great time to snag deals on accommodations and experience the cozy ambiance of Brussels without the crowds.

When planning your visit, it's worth checking for any major events or holidays that might impact your trip. Brussels hosts various cultural festivals, such as the Brussels Jazz Marathon in May and the Comic Strip Festival in September. These events add an extra layer of excitement to your visit and provide opportunities to immerse yourself in the local culture.

Ultimately, the best time to visit Brussels depends on your personal preferences, budget, and the experiences you wish to have. Whether you're exploring spring blossoms, enjoying summer festivities, embracing the winter wonderland, or indulging in autumn colors, Brussels has something to offer year-round.

So, my friend, consider your ideal weather, your desired activities, and the budget-friendly options available during different seasons. With a little planning and flexibility, you'll find the perfect time to visit Brussels and create unforgettable memories in this captivating city.

Budget-Friendly Travel Tips

Alright, my budget-savvy buddy, let's get down to business and talk about some killer tips to help you conquer Brussels without breaking the bank. We've got your back when it comes to accommodation, transportation, dining, and sightseeing. Get ready to stretch that hard-earned cash and make the most of your adventure!

Accommodation: When it comes to finding a place to crash, think beyond the fancy hotels. Brussels has a fantastic range of budget-friendly options. Hostels are a traveler's best friend, offering affordable dormitory beds and a chance to meet fellow adventurers. If you prefer a bit more privacy, check out guesthouses and budget hotels, especially those located slightly outside the city center. You'll find cozy spots without the hefty price tag.

Transportation: Getting around Brussels without breaking the bank? Challenge accepted! First off, ditch the taxis and embrace the city's excellent public transportation system. Buses and trams will zip you around town at a fraction of the cost. If you're planning to stay for a few days, consider getting a Brussels Card, which gives you unlimited access to public transport and free or discounted entry to various attractions. And don't forget, Brussels is a walking and cycling paradise, so put on those comfy shoes and hit the pavement!

Dining: Ah, the joy of sampling Belgian cuisine without emptying your wallet. Here's the scoop: street food is your best friend. Indulge in piping hot frites (Belgian fries) and delicious waffles from food stalls and carts scattered throughout the city. Believe me, your taste buds will appreciate you. Another tip is to seek out local markets, where you'll find fresh produce, cheese, and other goodies at reasonable prices. And if you're up for a sit-down meal, look for "Menu du Jour" or daily specials at restaurants, offering affordable set menus that won't leave your wallet crying.

Sightseeing: Brace yourself for some amazing sights without the jaw-dropping price tags. Brussels is packed with free and affordable attractions that will blow your mind. The iconic Grand Place is a must-see, and guess what? It won't cost you a dime to admire its stunning architecture. Take advantage of free museum days or opt for museums with discounted rates. Explore the city's parks and gardens, like the beautiful Parc du Cinquantenaire, where you can soak up nature's beauty without spending a cent. Oh, and keep an eye out for free walking tours, which provide a fantastic overview of the city's history and culture.

So, my savvy friend, armed with these budget-friendly travel tips, you're ready to conquer Brussels like a true money-saving pro. From smart accommodation choices to hopping on trams, devouring street food, and exploring the city's affordable attractions, you'll make every euro count. Get out there and create unforgettable memories without blowing your budget.

Brussels is waiting, and you're about to have the adventure of a lifetime!

Saving Money in Brussels

If you're looking to make every euro count during your time in Brussels, you've come to the right place. Let's dive into some awesome money-saving tips that will help you stretch your budget and have an epic time without burning through your wallet.

Explore on Foot or by Bike: Brussels is a compact city, perfect for exploring on foot or by bike. Skip the pricey transportation fares and take advantage of the city's pedestrian-friendly streets and dedicated cycling paths. Not only will you save money, but you'll also stumble upon hidden gems and experience the city's charm up close and personal.

Take Advantage of Free Attractions: Brussels has a wealth of free attractions that will blow your mind. From the jaw-dropping architecture of the Grand Place to the stunning views from Mont des Arts, you can soak up the city's beauty without spending a single cent. Explore the quirky Atomium from the outside, wander through the beautiful Parc du Cinquantenaire, and don't forget to visit the famous Manneken Pis, the little peeing statue that steals the show.

Seek Out Affordable Dining Options: While indulging in street food is a must, there are also affordable dining options to explore. Look for local eateries and small restaurants that offer "Menu du Jour" or daily specials. These set menus often come at a reasonable price and give you a taste of Belgian cuisine without emptying your wallet. Plus, don't forget to check out the local markets, where you can grab fresh produce, cheese, and other goodies to create your budget-friendly meals.

Research Discounts and Free Days: Many museums and attractions in Brussels offer discounted or free entry on specific days or times. Do your homework and plan your visits accordingly. Some museums even have specific days of the month when admission is completely free. Take advantage of these opportunities to explore the city's cultural offerings without spending a fortune.

Consider a Brussels Card: If you're planning to visit multiple attractions and use public transportation, it might be worth investing in a Brussels Card. This card offers unlimited access to public transport, free entry to various museums and attractions, and discounts at selected restaurants and shops. Do the math and see if the card aligns with your itinerary and budget.

Take Advantage of Happy Hour: Cheers to saving money! Brussels has a vibrant nightlife scene, and many bars and pubs offer happy hour specials. Keep an eye out for discounted drink prices and enjoy a night out without blowing your budget. It's a great way to mingle with locals and fellow travelers while sipping on some of Belgium's finest brews.

Shop Smart at Local Markets: Don't miss the local markets in Brussels, where you can find fresh produce, cheese, chocolates, and other goodies at reasonable prices. Stock up on snacks, picnic essentials, and souvenirs while supporting local vendors. It's a win-win!

By following these money-saving tips, you'll be able to explore Brussels on a budget without missing out on the city's incredible experiences.

Travel Insurance for Budget Travelers

When you're jetting off on an exciting adventure, the last thing you want to think about is the unexpected. But hey, life happens, right? That's where travel insurance comes in to save the day and ensure you have a worry-free journey without burning a hole in your wallet. Let's dive into the world of travel insurance for us budget-savvy travelers!

First things first, what exactly is travel insurance? Well, think of it as your ultimate safety net. It's like having a trusty sidekick that's got your back when things go awry during your trip. From medical emergencies to lost luggage or trip cancellations, travel insurance steps in to cover those unexpected mishaps and keeps you stress-free.

I can currently read your thoughts. "But won't travel insurance break the bank?" Fear not, my friend! There are budget-friendly options tailored just for us savvy travelers. Look out for insurance plans that offer essential coverage without the hefty price tag. Take the time to compare different providers and their offerings to find the best fit for your needs and budget.

When it comes to budget travel insurance, there are a few key things to consider. First, make sure your policy covers medical expenses. Trust me, having medical coverage can be a lifesaver when you find yourself in need of medical care abroad. It is dependably desirable to be protected than sorry!

Next up, check if the policy includes coverage for trip cancellation or interruption. Life is unpredictable and sometimes plans change. If your trip gets canceled or cut short due to unforeseen circumstances like illness or natural disasters, having this coverage will help you recoup your expenses and minimize any financial losses.

Lost or delayed baggage? No problem! Look for travel insurance that includes coverage for baggage and personal belongings. That way, if your luggage decides to take a detour or go on a little adventure of its own, you'll have peace of mind knowing you're covered.

Lastly, don't forget to read the fine print and understand the policy's limitations and exclusions. Each insurance plan has its own set of terms and conditions, so be sure to know what's covered and what's not. Ask questions if you're unsure about anything – it's always better to be well-informed.

So, my frugal friend, don't leave home without travel insurance. It's your secret weapon against unexpected bumps in the road. Look for budget-friendly options that provide essential coverage, including medical expenses, trip cancellation, lost baggage, and more. With the right travel insurance in your back pocket, you can explore the world with peace of mind, knowing you're protected without breaking the bank.

GETTING TO BRUSSELS

Getting to Brussels on a Budget

Alrighty, my adventurous friend! You've got Brussels on your radar, and you're ready to dive into the heart of this vibrant city. But wait, how do you get there without draining your wallet? Fear not, because I've got you covered with some budget-friendly ways to reach Brussels. Let's explore your options and get this adventure rolling!

By Air: If you're coming from afar or simply prefer the speed and convenience of air travel, hopping on a flight to Brussels can be a great option. Now, keep your eyes peeled for those sweet flight deals! Be flexible with your travel dates, and use flight comparison websites to snag the best prices. Remember, budget airlines often offer lower fares, but keep an eye out for extra fees and baggage restrictions. Pro tip: Consider flying into alternative airports near Brussels and take advantage of affordable ground transportation options to reach the city center.

By Train: All aboard the budget train to Brussels! Traveling by train can be a scenic and wallet-friendly way to reach the Belgian capital. If you're coming from neighboring countries like France, Germany, or the Netherlands, check out regional or international train connections. Look for discounted fares and special promotions, especially if you book your tickets in advance. Keep in mind that train travel may take a bit longer than flying, but hey, you get to enjoy the picturesque landscapes along the way. Plus, you'll arrive right in the heart of Brussels, ready to start your adventure!

By Bus: All right, buckle up for a road trip! Traveling by bus is a cost-effective option that allows you to soak up the scenery and make new friends along the way. There are several bus companies offering routes to Brussels from various European cities. Look for budget-friendly bus operators known for their affordable fares. Keep in mind that bus travel may take longer than other modes of transportation, but hey, time flies when you're having fun, right? Pro tip: Pack some snacks, load up your favorite playlist, and get ready for a comfortable journey on a budget.

No matter which mode of transportation you choose, make sure to compare prices, consider the travel time, and factor in any additional costs like baggage fees. Don't forget to stay updated on any travel restrictions or requirements, especially in these ever-changing times.

Whether you're soaring through the skies, chugging along on a train, or cruising on a budget-friendly bus, getting to Brussels doesn't have to break the bank. Choose the option that suits your budget, time frame, and sense of adventure. Now, go ahead and start planning your journey to the land of waffles, chocolate, and stunning architecture. Brussels is waiting for you with open arms!

Getting Around Brussels

Alright, you've made it to Brussels! Now it's time to navigate this incredible city and uncover all its hidden gems. Lucky for you, getting around Brussels doesn't have to be a budget buster. Let's dive into some fantastic ways to explore the city without breaking the bank. Get ready for a wallet-friendly transportation extravaganza!

Public Transportation: Brussels has an excellent public transportation system that will whisk you around the city with ease. The metro, buses, and trams are not only convenient but also affordable. Grab yourself a reusable transport card, such as the MOBIB card, and load it up with credits. This way, you can enjoy discounted fares and hop on and off as you please. Pro tip: Opt for day passes or multi-day passes if you plan on using public transportation extensively. It's a great way to save some cash while zipping around Brussels like a local!

Walking and Cycling: Lace up your walking shoes or hop on a bike because Brussels is a pedestrian and cyclist-friendly city! The compact city center makes it a joy to explore on foot. Marvel at the stunning architecture, stroll through charming neighborhoods and stumble upon delightful cafés and shops. If you're up for some two-wheeled adventures, Brussels offers bike-sharing services where you can rent a bike for a reasonable price. Pedal your way through the city's parks, along the canals, and immerse yourself in the vibrant atmosphere. Pro tip: Check out bike paths and dedicated cycling routes for a safer and more enjoyable experience.

Budget-Friendly Transportation Tips

Here are a few extra tips to keep your transportation costs in check while adventuring in Brussels:

Group Tickets: Traveling with friends? Consider purchasing group tickets for public transportation. Many cities offer discounted rates for groups, allowing you to split the cost and save some extra euros.

Free Walking Tours: Want to learn about Brussels' history and culture while getting your steps in? Join a free walking tour! These tours are led by knowledgeable locals who are passionate about their city. Not only will you get an insider's perspective, but you'll also have the chance to make new friends along the way.

Explore on Sundays: On Sundays, public transportation fares are often reduced, making it an excellent opportunity to plan your sightseeing adventures. Take advantage of this budget-friendly day and explore Brussels to your heart's content.

Shared Rides: If you're traveling with friends or fellow budget-savvy explorers, consider sharing rides with apps like UberPOOL or local ride-sharing services. Splitting the fare can make transportation more affordable while adding an element of socializing to your journey.

Remember, getting around Brussels on a budget doesn't mean compromising on your adventure. With a little planning and creativity, you can explore the city's captivating corners without emptying your wallet. So hop on a tram, stroll through the cobblestone streets, and immerse yourself in the vibrant atmosphere of Brussels.

BUDGET-FRIENDLY SIGHTS AND ACTIVITIES

Grand-Place on a Budget

The Grand-Place! A sight to behold, a marvel of architectural splendor, and the beating heart of Brussels. You might think that experiencing this iconic square comes with a hefty price tag, but fear not, my budget-savvy friend. I'm here to show you how to enjoy the Grand Place on a budget.

First and foremost, let me delight you with the news that entry to the Grand Place itself is free! That's right, you can wander through this architectural wonderland, gaze at the ornate guild halls, and soak up the vibrant atmosphere without spending a single penny. It's a feast for the eyes and a testament to Brussels' rich history.

To enhance your Grand Place experience without breaking the bank, consider visiting during different times of the day. Witness the changing light and atmosphere as the sun casts its magical glow on the square. Perhaps an early morning stroll or a visit during the enchanting twilight hours will reveal a different side of this iconic site.

While entry to the Grand Place is free, there are opportunities to spend a little to enhance your experience. Treat yourself to a coffee or a snack at one of the cafés surrounding the square. Indulge in a warm waffle topped with chocolate or savor a refreshing Belgian brew while taking in the incredible view. It's a budget-friendly way to immerse yourself in the ambiance and savor the moment.

Additionally, keep an eye out for special events and festivals that take place in the Grand Place throughout the year. From vibrant music performances to cultural celebrations, these events offer a chance to experience the square in a whole new light. Best of all, many of these events are free or have a nominal entry fee, making them accessible to all.

So, my budget-savvy friend, get ready to marvel at the Grand Place without emptying your wallet. Take in the awe-inspiring architecture, wander through the square, and soak up the vibrant atmosphere—all for free. Treat yourself to a coffee or snack, and if the timing aligns, catch a special event or festival. The Grand Place is yours to explore and enjoy without straining your budget. Happy discoveries!

Exploring Neighborhoods on a Budget

Brussels is a city of enchanting neighborhoods, each with its unique charm and character. From the historic streets of the Marolles to the trendy boutiques of Saint-Gilles, there's so much to discover beyond the tourist hotspots. The best part? You can explore these vibrant neighborhoods on a budget.

One of the simplest and most cost-effective ways to explore neighborhoods is by foot. Lace up your walking shoes and set off on a walking adventure. Wander through the winding streets, admire the colorful facades, and stumble upon quaint cafés, local markets, and hidden parks. It's the perfect opportunity to soak up the local atmosphere and get a feel for the city's vibrant neighborhoods.

Another budget-friendly option is to rent a bicycle. Brussels is a bike-friendly city with an extensive network of cycling paths. Renting a bike allows you to cover more ground and discover multiple neighborhoods in a single day. Pedal your way through the charming streets, visit local parks, and embrace the city's cycling culture. It's a fun and affordable way to experience Brussels from a different perspective.

When exploring neighborhoods on a budget, don't forget to embrace the local food scene. Seek out local markets, food stalls, and street vendors offering delicious and affordable treats. Indulge in a crispy cone of Belgian fries, savor a warm waffle topped with chocolate, or feast on a mouthwatering portion of moules-frites. Exploring neighborhoods on a budget doesn't mean sacrificing culinary delights.

Additionally, keep an eye out for free or low-cost cultural events happening in different neighborhoods. From art exhibitions to live music performances, Brussels has a vibrant cultural scene that often offers free or discounted entry to events. Check out local event listings, community centers, and cultural institutions to discover these hidden gems.

To make the most of your budget-friendly neighborhood exploration, consider joining a free walking tour. These tours, led by knowledgeable locals, offer insights into the history, architecture, and culture of various neighborhoods. Not only will you gain a deeper understanding of the city, but you'll also have the opportunity to connect with fellow travelers and make new friends along the way.

Lastly, don't be afraid to venture off the beaten path and explore lesser-known neighborhoods. Brussels is full of surprises, and sometimes the most memorable experiences can be found in the unassuming corners of the city. Get lost in the narrow streets, strike up conversations with locals, and let the neighborhoods reveal their hidden treasures.

So, my intrepid explorer, get ready to unveil Brussels' neighborhoods without breaking the bank. Whether you choose to wander on foot, pedal your way through on a bike, indulge in local delicacies, join a free walking tour, or venture off the beaten path, the vibrant neighborhoods of Brussels await.

Free and Affordable Museums

Calling all culture buffs! Brussels is home to a plethora of museums, each offering a fascinating glimpse into art, history, and the vibrant heritage of the city. The best part? Many of these cultural treasures can be explored for free or at an affordable price. Let's dive into the world of free and affordable museums in Brussels and embark on an enriching journey without emptying our wallets!

One of the most renowned museums in Brussels is the Royal Museums of Fine Arts. While the permanent collection may have an admission fee, mark your calendar for the first Wednesday of the month when entry is free. Immerse yourself in masterpieces by Belgian and international artists, and let the artistry ignite your imagination.

Another gem is the BELvue Museum, where you can dive into the history and culture of Belgium. This museum offers free admission to visitors under the age of 18, making it a family-friendly and budget-conscious choice. Explore interactive exhibits, delve into Belgium's past, and gain a deeper understanding of its rich heritage.

But wait, there's more! Brussels is a city that embraces its artistic and cultural side, and many museums offer free admission on specific days or times. Keep an eye out for the first Sunday of the month, when several museums open their doors to the public free of charge. From the Magritte Museum to the Museum of Natural Sciences, these institutions provide an opportunity to immerse yourself in art, science, and history without straining your budget.

For those seeking even more affordable cultural experiences, consider visiting lesser-known museums and galleries. Brussels is full of hidden cultural gems that often offer free or low-cost entry. From contemporary art spaces to specialized museums dedicated to topics like comics or music, there's something for every interest and budget.

Lastly, don't forget to check museum websites and local listings for temporary exhibitions or special events. These often come with separate ticket prices, but they provide an opportunity to explore specific themes or collections that align with your interests.

So, my cultural explorer, get ready to unleash Brussels' museums without breaking the bank. Immerse yourself in art and history at free and affordable museums, from the Royal Museums of Fine Arts to lesser-known cultural gems. Mark your calendar for free admission days or times, and keep an eye out for special exhibitions that pique your interest. Discover the rich heritage of Belgium, immerse yourself in artistic masterpieces, and expand your knowledge—all without straining your budget. Brussels' cultural treasures are waiting to be explored, so go forth and embark on an enriching journey through the city's museums!

Parks and Gardens

In the bustling city of Brussels, finding pockets of tranquility and green spaces is a breath of fresh air. Luckily, the city is adorned with a variety of parks and gardens that offer a welcome respite from the urban hustle. The best part? Enjoying the beauty and serenity of these outdoor spaces won't put a strain on your wallet. Let's explore the parks and gardens of Brussels, where nature's wonders await!

Brussels Park (Parc de Bruxelles) is a popular green park in the city. This sprawling park in the middle of the city provides a pleasant respite. Stroll along the tree-lined pathways, relax on the lush lawns, and take in the grandeur of the surrounding architecture. Whether you're looking for a spot to read a book, have a picnic, or simply unwind, Parc de Bruxelles is an oasis of tranquility.

For those seeking a more enchanting experience, head to the Botanical Garden of Brussels. This hidden gem invites you to wander through its lush gardens, discover a wide variety of plants, and take in the fragrance of blooming flowers. The entrance to the garden is free, allowing you to immerse yourself in nature's beauty without spending a penny. Pro tip: Check the garden's website for any guided tours or special events that may enhance your visit.

Another notable park is Parc du Cinquantenaire (Jubelpark), boasting vast green lawns, majestic statues, and a triumphal arch. It's an ideal spot for a stroll or a picnic with friends. Enjoy the tranquility, marvel at the architectural splendor, and soak up the sunshine on a budget-friendly outing.

But the parks and gardens of Brussels don't stop there. Bois de la Cambre, with its winding paths and serene lake, offers an escape to nature's embrace. Woluwe Park, with its picturesque lake and rolling landscapes, is perfect for a peaceful afternoon. And the charming Tenbosch Park is a hidden gem where you can unwind amidst beautiful flora.

So, lace up your walking shoes, pack a picnic, and get ready to embrace the beauty of Brussels' parks and gardens. From Parc de Bruxelles to the Botanical Garden and beyond, these budget-friendly havens offer a chance to connect with nature, find solace in green surroundings, and recharge your spirit. Discover hidden nooks, bask in the serenity, and let the wonders of nature uplift your soul—all without breaking the bank.

Self-Guided Walking Tours

Brussels is a city filled with fascinating history, captivating architecture, and hidden treasures. And what better way to explore its nooks and crannies than through self-guided walking tours? Whether you're a history buff, an architecture enthusiast, or simply a curious traveler, self-guided walking tours allow you to uncover Brussels' secrets at your own pace and on your terms. Let's embark on a journey of discovery as we walk through the charming streets of Brussels!

To begin your self-guided adventure, start at the heart of Brussels: the Grand Place.

Marvel at the ornate guildhalls, take in the stunning architecture and let the grandeur of this iconic square set the stage for your exploration. From there, you can choose from a variety of themed walking tours to suit your interests.

For history enthusiasts, a stroll through the historic center will transport you back in time. Discover the remnants of medieval Brussels as you meander through the narrow streets of the Marolles neighborhood, where antique shops and hidden gems await. Explore the rich heritage of the Sablon district, known for its elegant architecture and charming boutiques. And don't miss the chance to visit the iconic Manneken Pis statue and learn about its quirky history.

Architecture lovers will be in awe as they wander through Brussels' Art Nouveau neighborhoods. Admire the elegant facades, intricate ironwork, and organic motifs that define this artistic movement. Explore the Ixelles neighborhood, known for its stunning Art Nouveau houses, or head to the Schaerbeek district to uncover hidden architectural gems.

If you're interested in Brussels' culinary scene, a self-guided food tour is a must. Explore the city's markets, sample delicious treats like chocolate and waffles, and indulge in a traditional Belgian beer or two. Brussels' vibrant food culture is sure to leave your taste buds tingling with delight.

Don't forget to include the city's parks and green spaces in your walking tours. From the tranquil Parc de Bruxelles to the enchanting Botanical Garden, these outdoor oases provide a breath of fresh air and a chance to connect with nature amidst the bustling city.

To enhance your self-guided tours, arm yourself with a detailed map, either in print or on your phone, and keep an eye out for information panels or signage along the way. Many popular walking routes can be found online, offering valuable insights into the city's history, architecture, and culture.

So, put on your walking shoes, grab a map, and get ready to unveil the secrets of Brussels at your own pace. Whether you're exploring the historic center, delving into Art Nouveau districts, indulging in culinary delights, or wandering through lush parks, self-guided walking tours allow you to immerse yourself in the city's wonders. Take your time, follow your curiosity, and let the stories of Brussels unfold with each step you take.

Festivals and Events on a Budget

Brussels is a city that loves to celebrate, and luckily for budget-conscious travelers, many of its festivals and events offer a wealth of experiences without draining your wallet. From vibrant street parties to cultural celebrations, there's always something happening in Brussels that won't break the bank. Let's dive into the world of budget-friendly festivals and events that will make your trip to Brussels even more memorable!

The Flower Carpet is one of the most eagerly awaited events in Brussels. This biennial extravaganza transforms the Grand Place into a mesmerizing tapestry of flowers, creating a breathtaking sight. Best of all, entry to the Flower Carpet is free! Soak up the vibrant colors and floral fragrances as you explore this floral wonderland.

Comic strip enthusiasts will be delighted by the Brussels Comic Strip Festival. Held annually, this event celebrates the rich heritage of Belgian comics and showcases the works of renowned comic book artists. There's something for everyone, from exhibits to book signings. What's even better? Entry to many of the festival activities is free!

If you're visiting Brussels during the summer months, be sure to check out the Brussels Summer Festival. This multi-genre music festival takes place in various locations throughout the city and features both established and up-and-coming artists. While some concerts may require a ticket, the festival also offers free outdoor performances, You may enjoy street art and a colorful atmosphere for free. It's a fantastic opportunity to soak up the summer vibes and experience the city's music scene.

For those interested in cultural events, Brussels' museums often host free or discounted entry days during special occasions. From Museum Night Fever, where you can explore numerous museums after hours, to Museum Night in September, when museums stay open late and offer a range of activities, these events provide a unique and budget-friendly way to experience the city's cultural offerings.

Throughout the year, Brussels also hosts a variety of street parties and neighborhood festivals. From the Ommegang, a historical procession that reenacts a medieval pageant, to the Iris Festival, which celebrates the city's identity and diversity, these events showcase the vibrant spirit of Brussels. Join in the festivities, enjoy live music, dance to the rhythm, and indulge in delicious street food—all without straining your budget.

To keep track of the city's festivals and events, check local event listings, follow Brussels' tourism websites and social media channels, and keep an eye out for posters and flyers around the city. These resources will provide you with up-to-date information on upcoming events, dates, and any associated costs.

Alternative Attractions in Brussels

Brussels is a city of surprises, with a multitude of alternative attractions that offer unique experiences beyond the traditional tourist spots. If you're seeking something off the beaten path, away from the crowds, and a little bit different, then let's embark on a journey to uncover Brussels' hidden gems!

One such gem is the Atomium, an architectural marvel that stands tall and proud in the city. This iconic structure, designed to resemble an iron crystal, offers panoramic views of Brussels from its observation deck. Explore the exhibition halls inside, learn about its history, and marvel at the futuristic design. It's an alternative attraction that promises to leave you awestruck.

For those with a penchant for the arts, the Comic Strip Center is a must-visit. This museum celebrates the rich history and artistry of comic books, paying homage to Belgium's status as the birthplace of beloved characters like Tintin and the Smurfs.

Immerse yourself in the colorful world of comics, explore the exhibits, and indulge your inner child.

Venturing into Brussels' neighborhoods will reveal even more alternative attractions. Visit the Autoworld museum to satisfy your automotive curiosity, where a vast collection of vintage cars and iconic vehicles awaits. For music enthusiasts, a trip to the Musical Instruments Museum is a must. Explore its vast collection of instruments from around the world, and don't miss the chance to attend a live concert in its stunning concert hall.

Brussels is likewise home to an abundance of fantastic street art. Take a self-guided tour through neighborhoods like Saint-Gilles or Ixelles, where colorful murals adorn buildings, turning the city into an urban art gallery. Seek out the works of internationally renowned street artists or stumble upon hidden gems around unexpected corners.

Foodies will delight in Brussels' food markets, such as the popular Marché du Midi. Browse stalls brimming with fresh produce, local delicacies, and international flavors. Immerse yourself in

the lively atmosphere, sample street food, and embrace the vibrant culinary scene of the city.

Lastly, consider exploring Brussels' lesser-known neighborhoods. From the trendy and multicultural Matongé district to the vibrant and creative hub of Saint-Géry, these areas offer a glimpse into the city's diverse cultural fabric. Discover unique boutiques, cozy cafés, and independent art galleries that showcase the city's thriving creative scene.

To uncover these alternative attractions, do some research beforehand and tap into local recommendations. Check out online resources, ask locals for their favorite hidden spots, and keep an open mind as you explore the city. Sometimes the most memorable experiences are found where least expected.

WHERE TO EAT ON A BUDGET

Budget-Friendly Belgian Cuisine

Hey there, my friend! So you're ready to embark on a delicious journey through the world of budget-friendly Belgian cuisine? Excellent choice! Let's dive right in and explore some mouthwatering dishes that won't break the bank.

Belgian Fries: Crispy and golden, Belgian fries are a must-try when in Brussels. You can find them at numerous street food stalls throughout the city. Grab a cone of these perfectly cooked delights for around €2-€4, depending on the size and toppings. Don't forget to try them with a variety of sauces like mayonnaise, ketchup, or even the traditional "andalouse" sauce for an extra kick.

Waffles: Ah, waffles! These sweet treats are practically synonymous with Belgian cuisine. Indulge in a warm, freshly made waffle topped with powdered sugar or decadent chocolate sauce. You can find them at street food stalls, in cafes, or even at specialized waffle shops. Prices typically range from €2-€5, depending on the toppings and location.

Moules-Frites: If you're a fan of seafood, you can't miss out on trying moules-frites, a classic Belgian dish. Mussels steamed in white wine or beer served with a side of crispy fries—it's a match made in culinary heaven! Look for budget-friendly restaurants or brasseries where you can enjoy this dish for around €10-€15, depending on the portion size.

Carbonnade Flamande: This hearty Belgian beef stew cooked with beer and served with bread or fries is a true comfort food delight. Seek out traditional Belgian restaurants or taverns for a taste of this flavorful dish. Prices typically range from €10-€15, depending on the establishment.

Liège Waffles: As you continue your culinary adventure, be sure to try Liège waffles. These sweet treats are characterized by their caramelized sugar coating, giving them a delightful crunch. You can find them at street food stalls or specialized waffle shops for around €2-€5.

Speculoos: Don't forget to satisfy your sweet tooth with some delicious Belgian speculoos cookies. These spiced shortbread treats are perfect with a cup of coffee or as a snack on the go. Grab a pack from a local supermarket or bakery for just a few euros.

Belgian Chocolate: Last but certainly not least, indulge in the world-renowned Belgian chocolates. You'll find a wide variety of artisanal chocolate shops throughout Brussels. Treat yourself to a selection of pralines or truffles, and prepare for a taste sensation. Prices vary depending on the shop and the quantity but expect to spend around €5-€10 for a small box of exquisite chocolates.

Remember, my friend, these are just a few examples of the budget-friendly Belgian delights that await you. From fries and waffles to savory stews and mouth-watering chocolates, Brussels has a treasure trove of culinary experiences to offer. Prices may vary depending on the location and establishment, but with a little exploration, you'll find delicious options that won't strain your budget. So, go forth and indulge in the flavors of Belgium without breaking the bank. Bon appétit!

Cheap Eats in Brussels

When it comes to affordable and tasty options, Brussels' street food scene is a treasure trove. Wander through the streets and let your senses guide you to the tempting aromas and flavors of local delicacies. Indulge in a piping hot cone of Belgian fries, crispy on the outside and fluffy on the inside. Pair them with a dollop of tangy mayonnaise or one of the many delicious sauces available.

Another must-try street food delight is the warm, golden waffle. Whether you prefer it dusted with powdered sugar or adorned with chocolate, strawberries, or whipped cream, these delectable treats will transport your taste buds to bliss. And the best part? Street vendors offer these delights at budget-friendly prices.

For a savory option, seek out the Belgian classic of moules-frites, a generous serving of steamed mussels served with a side of crispy fries. This satisfying dish is not only a delight for seafood lovers but also a great value for your money. Explore the streets of Brussels and discover the many street food stalls and vendors offering these and other culinary delights.

Another way to experience budget-friendly Belgian cuisine is by visiting local markets. These bustling hubs of culinary delights offer a treasure trove of fresh produce, local delicacies, and authentic flavors. Not only can you stock up on affordable ingredients, but you can also savor the vibrant atmosphere and connect with the local food culture.

The Sunday Market at Gare du Midi is a popular choice, where you'll find an array of stalls selling everything from fruits and vegetables to cheese, bread, and cured meats. Explore the stands, chat with the vendors, and embrace the opportunity to taste and sample local treats. You can create your picnic basket filled with budget-friendly goodies from the market.

If you're looking to save even more money, consider visiting grocery stores to create your own budget-friendly Belgian culinary adventure. From local supermarkets to specialized food stores, Brussels has plenty of options to choose from. Pick up a selection of Belgian cheeses, cured meats, freshly baked bread, and some delicious chocolates. Create a picnic spread and head to one of Brussels' picturesque parks or green spaces to enjoy your gastronomic feast.

The Bois de la Cambre, Parc du Cinquantenaire, and the Botanical Garden are just a few examples of the many scenic spots where you can unwind and savor your culinary creations. Pack a blanket, bring along some refreshing beverages, and let the beauty of nature enhance your dining experience.

To find grocery stores, look for chains like Carrefour, Delhaize, or Colruyt, which offer a wide range of products at various price points. Don't forget to explore the aisles for local specialties like speculoos cookies, Belgian chocolates, or regional beers, which make for fantastic souvenirs or additions to your culinary adventures.

Top 6 Budget Restaurants and Cafes

Hey, Are you ready to discover some fantastic budget-friendly restaurants and cafes in Brussels? Great choice! Let's dive right in and explore six delightful spots where you can enjoy delicious meals without breaking the bank. From cozy cafes to casual eateries, Brussels has something to satisfy every craving and budget. Let's get started!

Chez Léon: Known as a Brussels institution, Chez Léon has been serving traditional Belgian cuisine since 1893. Located near the famous Manneken Pis statue, this restaurant offers a cozy atmosphere and a menu filled with Belgian classics like moules-frites (mussels and fries) and carbonnade flamande (beef stew). You'll find affordable options here, with main dishes typically ranging from €12-€18.

Maison Antoine: Craving some Belgian fries? Look no further than Maison Antoine, a legendary spot for this beloved street food. Located in the heart of Brussels, this no-frills friterie is a local favorite. Grab a cone of perfectly cooked fries and choose from a variety of sauces. Prices start at around €3 for a small cone, making it a tasty and budget-friendly option.

Café Belga: Situated in the vibrant Flagey neighborhood, Café Belga is a popular spot for locals and tourists alike. This trendy cafe offers a relaxed atmosphere, an extensive drink menu, and a range of affordable dishes. Whether you're looking for a hearty breakfast, a quick lunch, or a casual dinner, you'll find reasonably priced options here, with main courses ranging from €8-€15.

Tonton Garby: If you're in the mood for a mouthwatering sandwich, Tonton Garby is the place to be. Located near the vibrant Sainte-Catherine area, this cozy eatery specializes in gourmet sandwiches bursting with flavor. From classic combinations to creative twists, there's something for everyone. Prices for a delicious sandwich typically range from €5-€10, depending on the ingredients.

Pitaya: If you're craving some affordable and tasty Asian cuisine, Pitaya is a fantastic choice. Located near the Grand Place, this casual restaurant offers a menu filled with delicious

Thai street food dishes. From aromatic curries to flavorful stir-fries, Pitaya delivers bold flavors at affordable prices. You can enjoy a satisfying meal for around €10-€15.

Le Petit Vélo: This charming little cafe is tucked away in the trendy Saint-Gilles neighborhood. Le Petit Vélo offers a cozy and welcoming ambiance, making it the perfect spot for a leisurely breakfast or brunch. Indulge in freshly baked pastries, eggs made to order, and delicious coffee. Prices for a delightful breakfast or brunch range from €8-€15.

These are just a few examples of the budget-friendly restaurants and cafes that await you in Brussels. As you explore the city, keep an eye out for local eateries, daily specials, and lunch deals that offer great value for your money. From traditional Belgian cuisine to international flavors, Brussels has a diverse culinary scene that caters to every budget. So, grab a seat, savor the flavors, and enjoy the company of friends or fellow travelers. Bon appétit!

NIGHTLIFE AND ENTERTAINMENT ON A BUDGET

Affordable Bars and Pubs in Brussels

We all know that exploring a city's nightlife can be a blast, but it's even better when it doesn't drain your wallet. So, grab a seat, raise your glass, and let's discover some budget-friendly watering holes in Brussels that will keep your spirits high without breaking the bank!

Imagine walking into a cozy pub, where the warm glow of dim lights and the sound of laughter fills the air. You settle in and glance at the menu, and to your delight, you find a fantastic selection of Belgian beers at prices that won't leave you crying in your pint. It's a beer lover's paradise, my friend!

One such gem is Delirium Café, a legendary establishment with a mind-boggling collection of over 2,000 beers from around the world. It's like stepping into a beer lover's dreamland, where you can sample unique brews without breaking the bank.

Looking for a more laid-back vibe? Head to the Poechenellekelder tucked away near the famous Manneken Pis statue. This charming pub offers a cozy atmosphere and a wide range of Belgian beers, making it a perfect spot to unwind after a day of exploring the city.

Now, picture yourself sitting on an outdoor terrace, basking in the warm Brussels sunshine, and sipping on a refreshing drink. Café Belga, located in the trendy Flagey neighborhood, offers just that. Enjoy a cool pint or a refreshing cocktail while people-watching and soaking in the vibrant atmosphere of this hip area.

Brussels is known for its lively bar scene, and you'll find countless hidden gems as you wander through the city's charming streets. From quirky pubs to trendy bars, there's something for every taste and budget.

So, my friend, get ready to raise a glass and embark on an adventure through Brussels' affordable bars and pubs. Cheers to finding the perfect spot to unwind, make new friends and create memories that will last a lifetime. Remember to drink responsibly, savor the flavors, and enjoy the vibrant nightlife this city has to offer. Here's to an unforgettable and budget-friendly experience in Brussels!

Low-Cost Music Venues and Clubs

Brace yourself for a wild ride through the vibrant music scene in Brussels without putting a dent in your wallet. Get ready to dance, sing along, and immerse yourself in the low-cost music venues and clubs that'll have you grooving all night long. Let's dive in:

Bonnefooi: This hidden gem is a must-visit for music enthusiasts on a budget. Bonnefooi offers a variety of live music genres, including jazz, blues, funk, and more. The best part? Many of their shows are free or have a minimal cover charge, allowing you to enjoy great tunes without breaking the bank.

L'Archiduc: Step into L'Archiduc, a legendary Art Deco jazz bar that has been rocking Brussels since the 1930s. This cozy venue hosts live jazz performances, creating an intimate and soulful atmosphere. The cover charges are generally affordable, making it a go-to spot for jazz lovers looking for a memorable night out.

Madame Moustache: If you're up for an eclectic mix of music genres, Madame Moustache is the place to be. This quirky venue hosts live bands, DJs, and themed nights ranging from rock to electronic and everything in between. The cover charges are usually reasonable, and the energetic vibe will keep you dancing until the early hours.

Café Central: Prepare yourself for a melting pot of musical styles at Café Central. This underground venue features a diverse lineup of live performances, including experimental, electronic, and alternative music. With its intimate setting and affordable entrance fees, Café Central is a go-to spot for music lovers seeking unique sounds.

Bar du Matin: Looking for a cozy spot to enjoy live acoustic performances? Bar du Matin is your answer. This intimate bar hosts regular live music sessions featuring local artists. Grab a drink, sit back, and let the soothing sounds of acoustic melodies wash over you.

With these low-cost music venues and clubs, you can experience the pulsating beats and incredible talent of Brussels' music scene without breaking the bank. So, let loose, sing your heart out, and dance like nobody's watching. Get ready for unforgettable nights filled with rhythm and good vibes. Enjoy the music, my friend, and let the melodies guide you on a budget-friendly musical journey in Brussels!

Alternative Nighttime Activities

So, you're looking for alternative nighttime activities that won't break the bank, huh? Well, you're in for a treat because Brussels has a vibrant nightlife scene that goes beyond the typical clubs and bars. Let's dive into some unique and budget-friendly activities to keep you entertained after the sun sets.

Nighttime Walking Tours: Ever wondered what the city looks like when the moon casts its magical glow? Join a nighttime walking tour and explore Brussels' enchanting streets under the stars. You'll uncover hidden gems, hear fascinating stories, and experience the city in a whole new light (literally!). It's like being part of a secret adventure!

Open-Air Movie Screenings: Picture this: a warm summer evening, a cozy blanket, and a classic movie playing under the open sky. Brussels hosts various open-air movie screenings throughout the year, offering a unique and budget-friendly way to enjoy cinema. Grab a picnic blanket, some popcorn, and get ready for a movie night under the stars. It's like a cinema experience on a celestial stage!

Evening Canal Cruises: Why not take a leisurely boat ride along Brussels' picturesque canals at night? Hop on an evening canal cruise and let the gentle water carry you through the city's illuminated sights. As you glide along, you'll witness stunning reflections, architectural marvels, and a serene ambiance that will leave you mesmerized. It's like sailing through a dreamy watercolor painting!

Night Markets and Events: Keep an eye out for special nighttime markets and events happening in Brussels. These lively gatherings often feature food stalls, live music, and local artisans. It's a fantastic opportunity to immerse yourself in the local culture, mingle with locals, and indulge in delicious treats without breaking the bank. It's like a nocturnal carnival of flavors and sounds!

Stargazing in Parks: Brussels has several parks where you can enjoy a peaceful evening of stargazing. Find a cozy spot, lay back, and marvel at the twinkling constellations above. It's a serene and awe-inspiring experience that reconnects you with the wonders of the universe. It's like having a personal cosmic show just for you!

My adventurous friend, step out of the ordinary and explore these alternative nighttime activities in Brussels. Whether you're on a budget or simply seeking something different, these experiences will create magical memories without putting a strain on your wallet. Embrace the night, unleash your curiosity, and let the city surprise you with its after-dark wonders. Happy nocturnal adventures!

WHERE TO STAY ON A BUDGET

Finding Budget Hotels and Hostels

Are you ready to uncover some fantastic options for affordable accommodation in Brussels? Great choice! Let's dive right in and discover how you can find budget-friendly hotels and hostels that will keep your wallet happy while providing a comfortable stay.

When it comes to budget hotels, Brussels offers a variety of options that cater to the needs of budget-conscious travelers. Look for centrally located hotels in neighborhoods like Sainte-Catherine, Saint-Gilles, or the European Quarter. These areas often have a range of affordable hotels that offer comfortable rooms and convenient access to the city's attractions. Prices for budget hotels in Brussels typically start at around €50 per night, depending on the location, amenities, and time of year.

If you're looking to connect with fellow travelers and save even more money, consider staying in a hostel. Brussels has a vibrant hostel scene, with options to suit every budget and preference. Hostels often provide dormitory-style rooms, private rooms, and communal areas where you can meet other travelers. Some popular hostels in Brussels include Meininger Brussels City Center, 2GO4 Quality Hostel Brussels Grand Place, and Brussels Hello Hostel. Prices for hostel stays typically start at around €15-€30 per night, depending on the room type and the time of year.

To find the best deals on accommodation, consider using online booking platforms that allow you to compare prices and read reviews from fellow travelers. Websites like Booking.com, Hostelworld, and Airbnb are great resources to find budget-friendly options that fit your needs.

Remember to book in advance, especially during peak travel seasons, to secure the best rates and availability. Additionally, keep an eye out for special promotions or last-minute deals that can offer additional savings.

With a wide range of budget hotels and hostels available, you can find comfortable and affordable accommodation that allows you to make the most of your trip. Choose a centrally located hotel or a vibrant hostel, connect with fellow travelers, and enjoy the convenience and comfort of your temporary home away from home. Happy travels!

Affordable Bed and Breakfasts

If you're looking for a cozy and affordable place to stay in Brussels, bed and breakfasts are the way to go. They offer a warm and welcoming atmosphere, personalized service, and a delightful start to your day with a delicious breakfast. Let's explore some fantastic options that won't break the bank!

La Maison Haute: Located in the heart of Brussels' historic center, La Maison Haute is a charming bed and breakfast that combines comfort and convenience. The cozy rooms and friendly hosts make you feel right at home. Rates for a double room start at around €70 per night, offering excellent value for money. With its central location, you'll have easy access to the city's iconic attractions, such as the magnificent Grand Place and the famous Manneken Pis statue.

B&B Les Clarisses: Nestled in the Sablon district, B&B Les Clarisses offers a serene escape in a beautiful historic setting. The tranquil ambiance and comfortable rooms provide a peaceful retreat after a day of exploration. Rates for a double room start at approximately €90 per night. You'll be within walking distance of attractions like the Royal Palace and the renowned Magritte Museum, allowing you to immerse yourself in the city's vibrant cultural scene.

Le Lys d'Or: Located in the lively Saint-Gilles neighborhood, Le Lys d'Or combines comfort with a touch of elegance. The cozy rooms and personalized service make for a delightful stay. Rates for a double room start at around €80 per night. This neighborhood is known for its vibrant atmosphere, trendy shops, and delicious restaurants. Don't forget to start your day with a scrumptious breakfast before venturing out to explore the city.

B&B La Maison de Margot: Situated in the vibrant Ixelles neighborhood, B&B La Maison de Margot offers a home away from home. The welcoming ambiance and comfortable accommodations ensure a pleasant stay. Rates for a double room start at approximately €75 per night. You'll be within walking distance of the lively Place Flagey, where you can immerse yourself in the local culture, dine at charming cafés, and enjoy a vibrant atmosphere.

B&B Taptoe: Just a stone's throw away from the famous Grand Place, B&B Taptoe is a delightful retreat in the heart of Brussels. The cozy rooms and central location make it an ideal choice for exploring the city. Rates for a double room start at around €85 per night. You'll be steps away from the city's major attractions, allowing you to immerse yourself in the historic charm and beauty of Brussels.

These affordable bed and breakfasts in Brussels offer a personal touch and a comfortable stay without straining your budget. Whether you're seeking a central location, a peaceful retreat, or a neighborhood with a vibrant atmosphere, you'll find a charming and affordable option that suits your preferences. So, choose the one that speaks to you, enjoy a delightful breakfast, and make the most of your stay in the fascinating city of Brussels.

Alternative Accommodation Options

If you're looking for alternative accommodation options that go beyond traditional hotels and hostels, Brussels has some fantastic choices that will suit your budget and add a unique touch to your travel experience. Let's explore a few alternative options that will make your stay in Brussels extra special!

Guesthouses: If you're seeking a more personalized and cozy experience, guesthouses are a wonderful choice. These accommodations often offer comfortable rooms, delicious breakfasts, and a warm and welcoming atmosphere. You can find guesthouses in various neighborhoods of Brussels, each with its charm and character. These alternative options provide an opportunity to connect with local hosts, receive insider tips, and enjoy a more intimate experience.

Apartments and Vacation Rentals: Renting an apartment or vacation rental can be an excellent choice for budget travelers, especially if you're traveling with a group or planning an extended stay. Websites like Airbnb offer a wide range of affordable options, from cozy studios to spacious apartments, allowing you to live like a local during your time in Brussels. With a kitchenette or full kitchen, you can also save money by preparing your meals with ingredients from local markets.

Homestays and Couchsurfing: For a truly immersive and budget-friendly experience, consider homestays or Couchsurfing. These options allow you to stay with residents, providing a unique opportunity to connect with the local culture, make new friends, and gain insider knowledge about Brussels. Homestays often involve a small fee, while Couchsurfing is based on the concept of free accommodation in exchange for cultural exchange and friendship.

House Sitting: If you're open to a longer-term stay and enjoy taking care of pets or maintaining a home, house sitting can be a fantastic option. Websites like TrustedHousesitters connect travelers with homeowners who need their houses and pets looked after while they're away. In exchange for your services, you get to stay in the homeowner's house for free, offering a budget-friendly and immersive experience.

These alternative accommodation options provide budget travelers with a range of choices to suit their preferences and add a unique touch to their Brussels adventure. Whether you opt for a cozy guesthouse, a private apartment, a homestay, or even house sitting, you'll find options that offer comfort, affordability, and a chance to connect with the local culture.

Tips for Booking Budget Accommodation

When it comes to booking budget accommodation in Brussels, there are a few handy tips and tricks that can help you find the best deals and stretch your travel budget even further. Let's explore some fantastic tips for booking budget-friendly accommodation:

Plan and book in advance: Booking your accommodation well in advance can often save you money. By planning, you can take advantage of early bird discounts, and promotional offers, and secure the best available rates. Plus, you'll have a wider range of options to choose from.

Be flexible with your travel dates: If your travel dates are flexible, try adjusting them to take advantage of off-peak seasons or weekdays when prices tend to be lower. Avoiding peak travel times and holidays can significantly reduce accommodation costs.

Use online booking platforms and comparison sites: Websites like Booking.com, Expedia, and Airbnb offer a wide range of accommodation options and allow you to compare prices, read reviews, and find the best deals. Take advantage of user-friendly filters to narrow down your search based on price, location, and amenities.

Consider alternative accommodation options: Think beyond traditional hotels and explore alternative options like guesthouses, bed and breakfasts, apartments, and even hostels. These alternatives often offer budget-friendly rates, unique experiences, and a chance to connect with locals.

Check for special promotions and discounts: Keep an eye out for special promotions, discounts, and package deals offered by hotels or booking platforms. Many establishments offer seasonal promotions, last-minute deals, or exclusive discounts for members.

Read reviews and ratings: Before booking accommodation, take the time to read reviews and ratings from previous guests. This can give you valuable insights into the quality, cleanliness, and overall experience of the property. Look for properties with positive reviews and high ratings to ensure a comfortable stay.

Consider location and transportation: Accommodation located in the city center or near public transportation can save you money on transportation costs and allow for convenient exploration of the city. However, if you're willing to stay a bit further from the main attractions, you might find more affordable options with easy access to public transportation.

Join loyalty programs: If you frequently travel or plan to visit Brussels multiple times, consider joining hotel loyalty programs. These programs often provide exclusive discounts, rewards, and perks that can make your stays more affordable and enjoyable.

Keep in mind, while booking budget accommodation is essential, always prioritize safety, cleanliness, and comfort. By following these tips and doing a little research, you'll be well on your way to finding budget-friendly accommodation in Brussels that meets your needs and allows you to make the most of your travel budget. Happy booking and enjoy your budget-friendly adventure in Brussels!

BUDGET SHOPPING AND SOUVENIRS

Budget-Friendly Shopping Tips

Are you looking to indulge in some retail therapy while keeping your budget intact, Brussels has plenty of opportunities for budget-friendly shopping. Here are some handy tips to help you score great deals and make the most of your shopping experience:

Explore local markets: Brussels is known for its vibrant markets where you can find a wide range of products at affordable prices. From fresh produce and local delicacies to unique crafts and vintage items, markets like the Brussels Midi Market and the Place du Jeu de Balle flea market offer budget-friendly shopping experiences with a touch of local flavor.

Take advantage of sales and discounts: Keep an eye out for sales and discounts happening in the city. Many shops and boutiques offer seasonal promotions, clearance sales, or special discounts during certain times of the year. Sign up for newsletters or follow your favorite stores on social media to stay updated on the latest deals.

Shop at outlet stores: Brussels is home to several outlet stores where you can find branded and designer items at discounted prices. Places like Maasmechelen Village and L'Esplanade in Louvain-la-Neuve offer a range of fashion, accessories, and home goods from popular brands at lower prices.

Embrace second-hand shopping: Thrift stores and consignment shops can be a treasure trove of unique and affordable finds. Brussels has a variety of thrift stores where you can discover pre-loved clothing, accessories, and home goods at bargain prices. Not only will you save money, but you'll also be supporting sustainable fashion practices.

Shop around and compare prices: Before making a purchase, compare prices at several stores and online platforms. Use price comparison websites and apps to guarantee you're receiving the greatest bargain possible. Don't be afraid to negotiate prices, especially in local markets or smaller shops where bargaining is common.

Set a budget and prioritize your purchases: Before you start shopping, set a budget to avoid overspending. Make a list of the items you need or prioritize the ones you want. This will help you stay focused and make thoughtful purchases, ensuring you get the most value for your money.

VAT refund: If you're a non-European Union resident, don't forget to inquire about the VAT refund program. You may be eligible to receive a refund on the value-added tax paid on your purchases. Just make sure to keep the necessary paperwork and follow the refund process before leaving the country.

By following these budget-friendly shopping tips, you can indulge in retail therapy without breaking the bank. Whether you're exploring local markets, taking advantage of sales, or embracing second-hand finds, Brussels offers plenty of options to satisfy your shopping cravings while keeping your wallet happy. So, put on your shopping shoes and get ready to find some fantastic deals in the wonderful city of Brussels. Happy shopping!

Markets and Flea Markets

Get ready to embark on a shopping adventure in Brussels, where markets and flea markets are a treasure trove of unique finds and local flavors. Whether you're hunting for fresh produce, one-of-a-kind antiques, or vintage clothing, the markets in Brussels offer a delightful experience for every budget traveler. Here's a glimpse into the vibrant world of markets and flea markets in the city.

Brussels boasts a variety of markets that cater to different tastes and interests. The Brussels Midi Market, one of the largest markets in Europe, is a bustling hub where you can find everything from fruits, vegetables, and flowers to clothing, accessories, and household items. It's the perfect spot to immerse yourself in the vibrant atmosphere and pick up some affordable goodies.

If you're a fan of vintage treasures and hidden gems, the Place du Jeu de Balle flea market is a must-visit. Located in the charming Marolles neighborhood, this market is known for its eclectic mix of antiques, second-hand items, and curiosities. Whether you're on the hunt for vintage clothing, antique furniture, or quirky collectibles, the market offers an exciting array of choices.

Another popular market worth exploring is the Sunday Market at Gare du Midi. This colorful market brings together vendors selling a variety of products, including artisanal crafts, clothing, jewelry, and delicious street food. It's a fantastic place to immerse yourself in the local culture, sample tasty treats, and discover unique souvenirs to take home.

When visiting these markets, don't forget to bring your bargaining skills. Many vendors are open to negotiation, so don't be afraid to haggle for a better price. It's all part of the fun and adds to the authentic market experience.

So, lace up your walking shoes, bring along your shopping bags, and get ready to explore the vibrant markets and flea markets of Brussels. From fresh produce to vintage treasures, these lively hubs offer a budget-friendly shopping experience where you can discover hidden gems and indulge in the local culture. Happy hunting and enjoy your market adventure in Brussels!.

Outlet Shopping in Brussels

Looking for incredible deals on branded and designer items? Look no further than outlet shopping in Brussels! This city is home to several outlet stores where you can find your favorite brands at discounted prices. Whether you're in search of fashion, accessories, or home goods, outlet shopping is a budget-friendly way to indulge in a little retail therapy.

Maasmechelen Village is a popular destination for outlet shopping, located just outside of Brussels. This charming open-air shopping village offers a wide range of high-end brands, including clothing, footwear, accessories, and more. Stroll through the picturesque streets and discover fantastic deals on luxury items.

L'Esplanade in Louvain-la-Neuve is another excellent outlet shopping destination near Brussels. With a mix of fashion, sportswear, and home goods stores, this shopping center offers discounted prices on popular brands, making it a favorite among savvy shoppers.

Outlet shopping in Brussels allows you to score significant discounts, often up to 70% off the original retail prices. It's a great opportunity to find quality items at a fraction of the cost, making your shopping budget go further.

So, if you're looking to upgrade your wardrobe, snag some designer accessories, or revamp your home decor without breaking the bank, head to the outlet stores in Brussels. With their wide selection of discounted items, you'll be able to shop to your heart's content while enjoying significant savings.

Souvenirs on a Budget

When it comes to bringing home a piece of Brussels as a souvenir, you'll be delighted to know that there are plenty of budget-friendly options that capture the essence of the city.

Here are some wonderful souvenirs on a budget that you can consider:

Chocolates: Belgium is renowned for its delicious chocolates, and they make perfect souvenirs. Look for local chocolatiers or visit chocolate shops where you can find a wide variety of affordable chocolate treats packaged beautifully. From pralines to truffles, these sweet delights will surely satisfy your taste buds and make great gifts for friends and family.

Belgian Beer: Belgium is also famous for its rich brewing tradition, so why not bring back some Belgian beer as a souvenir? Look for smaller, local breweries where you can find a wide range of affordable and unique beer options. Consider picking up a couple of bottles or a sampler pack to try different flavors and styles.

Waffles: Brussels is synonymous with mouthwatering waffles, and they can be a delightful and affordable Souvenir. Look for local street vendors or small bakeries where you can grab freshly made waffles at a reasonable price. Enjoy them on the go or bring some back for your loved ones to enjoy.

Lace Products: Belgium is known for its delicate lacework, and lace products make for elegant and unique souvenirs. Look for lace accessories like bookmarks, handkerchiefs, or small lace trinkets that can be found at local markets or specialty shops. They make for lovely keepsakes that showcase Belgian craftsmanship.

Comic Books: Belgium has a rich comic book culture, with famous characters like Tintin and The Smurfs originating from here. Consider picking up a comic book or graphic novel as a souvenir, which can be found in various price ranges depending on the edition and condition.

Postcards and Magnets: For a more traditional and budget-friendly option, grab some postcards or magnets featuring iconic landmarks of Brussels. They are easy to find at souvenir shops and make great mementos to share with friends and family.

Have in mind, the best souvenirs are the ones that hold special meaning to you. Choose items that resonate with your experience and capture the spirit of Brussels. By opting for these budget-friendly souvenirs, you can bring a piece of the city back home without breaking the bank. Happy souvenir shopping!

DAY TRIPS ON A BUDGET

Budget-Friendly Day Trips from Brussels

Hey there, my friend! Let's talk about some fantastic budget-friendly day trips you can take from Brussels. Brussels is not only a vibrant city itself but also a perfect starting point to explore the beauty of Belgium. So, grab your backpack, put on your comfy shoes, and get ready to embark on these exciting adventures!

Ghent: Just a short train ride away from Brussels, Ghent is a picturesque city with a rich history and stunning architecture. Explore the medieval city center, stroll along the canals, and marvel at the impressive Ghent Altarpiece. Don't forget to try the local specialty, Ghent's famous cuberdon candies. The best part? Ghent is budget-friendly, with affordable dining options and free attractions like Graslei and Korenlei.

Bruges: Known as the "Venice of the North," Bruges is a charming medieval city that will transport you back in time. Wander through its cobblestone streets, visit the iconic Markt Square, and take a boat ride along the canals. Don't miss the opportunity to try the delectable Belgian chocolates and indulge in some world-famous Belgian fries. Bruges may attract many tourists, but you can still find affordable places to eat and explore, especially if you venture off the main tourist paths.

Antwerp: If you're a fashion enthusiast or an art lover, Antwerp is a must-visit destination. This vibrant city is known for its fashion scene, diamond district, and impressive cultural heritage. Visit the Antwerp Cathedral, stroll along the trendy neighborhood of Het Zuid, and explore the fashion district of Meir. Enjoy a budget-friendly meal at a local café or grab a quick bite from one of the street food stands scattered around the city.

Waterloo: History buffs will find Waterloo intriguing as it was the site of the famous Battle of Waterloo. Explore the battlefield, visit the visitor center, and learn about the historic events that unfolded here. Take a moment to reflect and imagine the intense battle that took place. Admission fees may apply, but it's worth the experience to immerse yourself in history.

Leuven: Known for its vibrant student life, Leuven is a charming university town just a short train ride from Brussels. Explore the historic center, visit the iconic Leuven Town Hall, and don't miss the opportunity to try the local specialty beer, Stella Artois. Enjoy a budget-friendly picnic in one of the city's parks or grab a bite at one of the student-friendly eateries.

These budget-friendly day trips offer a fantastic opportunity to explore the beauty and diversity of Belgium. From the medieval charm of Ghent and Bruges to the vibrant culture of Antwerp and Leuven, there's something for everyone. So, pack your sense of adventure and get ready to make unforgettable memories on these budget-friendly excursions. Happy travels!

Budget-Friendly Transportation Options

When it comes to getting around Brussels on a budget, several transportation options won't break the bank. Let's explore these budget-friendly modes of transportation and their rates:

Public Transportation

Brussels has an efficient and affordable public transportation system consisting of buses, trams, and metros. The rates for a single journey within the city center start at around €2.10. However, if you plan to use public transportation frequently, consider purchasing a multi-day pass or a MOBIB card, which offers discounted fares for multiple journeys. A 24-hour pass costs approximately €7.50, while a 72-hour pass costs around €18.50.

Walking and Cycling

Brussels is a compact city that is easy to explore on foot or by bicycle. Walking is not only budget-friendly but also a great way to immerse yourself in the city's charm. There are numerous walking paths and pedestrian-friendly streets throughout the city. If you prefer cycling, you can rent a bicycle from Villo!, Brussels' bike-sharing service. Rates start at around €1.60 for 30 minutes.

Shared Mobility Services

Brussels offers various shared mobility options like electric scooters and shared cars, which can be a convenient and cost-effective way to get around the city. Popular scooter-sharing services such as Lime, Dott, and Troty have per-minute rates that range from €0.15 to €0.30. For shared cars, services like Cambio and Zipcar offer hourly rates starting from around €4, including fuel and insurance.

Taxis and Ridesharing

While taxis are generally more expensive than other modes of transportation, they can still be an option for short trips or when traveling in groups. Taxis in Brussels operate on a metered fare system, with an initial fee of around €3.50, and an additional charge per kilometer. Ridesharing services like Uber and Bolt are also available in Brussels, offering competitive rates compared to traditional taxis.

By utilizing these budget-friendly transportation options, you can navigate Brussels without putting a strain on your wallet. Whether you choose to explore the city on foot, take advantage of public transportation, or opt for shared mobility services, you'll find that getting around Brussels doesn't have to be expensive. So, hop on a tram, pedal your way through the city, or take a stroll, and enjoy your budget-friendly adventures in Brussels!

BUDGET TRAVEL RESOURCES

Budget Travel Websites and Apps

There are several budget travel websites and apps that can be incredibly useful for budget travelers. Here is a list of some of the recent ones:

Skyscanner: Skyscanner is a popular travel website and app that helps you find the best deals on flights, hotels, and car rentals. It allows you to compare prices across different airlines and travel agencies, ensuring you get the most affordable options.

Kayak: Kayak is another comprehensive travel search engine that helps you find budget-friendly flights, hotels, and rental cars. It also offers features like price alerts and flexible date searches to help you find the best deals.

Hopper: Hopper is a mobile app that predicts flight and hotel prices and notifies you when prices drop. It can help you save money by recommending the best time to book your travel arrangements.

Airbnb: Airbnb is a popular online marketplace for booking accommodations. It offers a wide range of budget-friendly options, including private rooms and entire apartments, allowing you to experience local culture while staying within your budget.

Hostelworld: Hostelworld is a website and app specifically designed for budget travelers looking for affordable accommodations such as hostels and budget hotels. It provides detailed information, reviews, and booking options for a variety of budget-friendly accommodations worldwide.

Rome2rio: Rome2rio is a multi-modal transport search engine that helps you plan your route and find the most cost-effective ways to travel between destinations. It provides information on various transportation options, including flights, trains, buses, and ferries.

Trail Wallet: Trail Wallet is a travel expense tracking app that helps you manage your budget while on the go. It allows you to set a daily spending limit, track your expenses, and categorize them, ensuring you stay within your budget throughout your trip.

These budget travel websites and apps can be invaluable tools for finding affordable flights, accommodations, and transportation options, as well as managing your travel expenses. They are constantly evolving to provide travelers with the best deals and information, making it easier than ever to explore the world on a budget.

Money-Saving Tips for Budget Travelers

As a budget traveler, it's important to find ways to save money without compromising on the quality of your travel experience. Here are money-saving tips to help you make the most of your budget:

Plan and Research in Advance: Planning is key to saving money. Research destinations, accommodations, and attractions in advance to find the best deals and discounts. Look for off-season travel opportunities when prices are lower, and consider flexible travel dates to take advantage of cheaper flights and accommodations.

Remain nearby - Couchsurfing interfaces you with local people who can give you a free spot to remain. In addition to the fact that it sets aside your cash yet, they can share their insider tips with you as well. It's the most effective way to interface with a neighborhood while setting aside cash.

Take a free strolling visit - Free strolling visits are the most ideal way to see the city on a careful spending plan. Simply make sure to tip your aid toward the end!

Visit exhibition halls when they are free - Numerous historical centers offer free passage on the principal Sunday of the month. Assuming you time your visit, you can exploit this and save a few euros. A portion of the galleries that offer this are the Brussels Historical Center of The Obstruction, the Unconstrained Craftsmanship Exhibition Hall, the Belgian Gallery of Freemasonry, the Jewish Gallery of Belgium, and the Brussels Historical Center of Industry and Work.

Eat Like a Local: One of the best ways to save money while traveling is by eating like a local. Explore local markets, street food stalls, and affordable restaurants to try authentic cuisine without breaking the bank. Avoid touristy areas where prices tend to be higher and opt for local dishes and specialties.

Use Public Transportation: Public transportation is often more cost-effective than taxis or rental cars. Research the public transportation options available in your destination and take advantage of discounted passes or travel cards. It's a great way to explore the city like a local and save money on transportation costs.

Bring a water bottle - The regular water here is protected to drink so bring a reusable water container to set aside cash and diminish your plastic use. LifeStraw is my go-to mark as their jugs have underlying channels to guarantee your water is in every case spotless and safe.

Remember, budget travel is all about finding a balance between cost-saving measures and enjoying your travel experience. By planning, making savvy choices, and embracing local culture, you can make the most of your budget and create unforgettable memories on your journey.

Language and Communication Tips

When visiting Brussels, it's helpful to have some language and communication tips to enhance your travel experience. While many people in Brussels speak English, making an effort to learn a few basic phrases and understanding the local customs can go a long way. Here are some language and communication tips for travelers visiting Brussels:

Learn Basic French and Dutch Phrases: Brussels is a bilingual city with both French and Dutch being official languages. Learning a few simple phrases like greetings, thank you, please, and basic questions in both languages can show respect and help you connect with locals.

Start with Greetings: When interacting with locals, begin with a polite greeting such as "Bonjour" (French) or "Goedendag" (Dutch), depending on the language preference. It sets a friendly tone and shows that you're making an effort to communicate.

Use English When Needed: While attempting to speak French or Dutch is appreciated, if you're struggling, it's perfectly fine to switch to English. Many people in Brussels have a good command of English, especially in tourist areas, hotels, and restaurants.

Be Polite and Courteous: Politeness and courtesy go a long way in any language. Saying "s'il vous plaît" (please) and "merci" (thank you) can make your interactions more pleasant. It's also good practice to learn basic etiquette and customs, such as greeting with a handshake and using formal titles when appropriate.

Utilize Translation Apps or Phrasebooks: If you're unsure about certain phrases or need translation assistance, consider using translation apps like Google Translate or carrying a pocket phrasebook. These tools can help you communicate effectively and overcome language barriers.

Seek Local Recommendations: Don't be afraid to ask locals for recommendations on places to visit, eat, or explore. Engaging in conversation with locals can provide valuable insights and make your experience more authentic.

Respect Cultural Differences: Each culture has its customs and norms. Take the time to familiarize yourself with the local customs and be respectful of them. This includes understanding dining etiquette, appropriate attire, and respecting personal space.

Have in mind, the key is to make an effort and show respect for the local language and culture. Even a few basic phrases can make a difference in your interactions and help you connect with the people of Brussels. Enjoy your time in the city and embrace the opportunity to immerse yourself in the rich cultural heritage of Brussels!

Basic French Vocabulary for Communication

Ready to brush up on some basic French vocabulary to enhance your communication skills in Brussels? It's time to charm the locals with a few handy phrases that will make navigating the city a breeze. Let's dive in and get you speaking French like a pro (or at least like a friendly traveler)!

1. Greetings:

- Bonjour (bohn-zhoor) - Hello
- Merci (mehr-see) - Thank you
- S'il vous plaît (see voo play) - Please
- Excusez-moi (ehk-skoo-zay mwah) - Excuse me

2. Introductions:

- Je m'appelle... (zhuh mah-pehl) - My name is...
- Comment ça va? (koh-mah sah vah) - How are you?
- Enchanté(e) (ahn-shahn-tey) - Nice to meet you

3. Common Phrases:

- Parlez-vous anglais? (par-lay voo ahn-glay) - Do you speak English?

- Où est...? (oo ay) - Where is...?

- Je ne comprends pas (zhuh nuh kohm-prahn pah) - I don't understand

- Combien ça coûte? (kohm-byahn sah koot) - What does it cost?

4. Ordering Food and Drinks:

- Une table pour un, s'il vous plaît (ewn tah-bl poor uh, see voo play) - A table for one, please

- Je voudrais... (zhuh voo-dreh) - I would like...

- L'addition, s'il vous plaît (lah-dee-syohn, see voo play) - The bill, please

5. Directions:

- À gauche (ah gohsh) - To the left
- À droite (ah dwaht) - To the right

- Tout droit (toot dwah) - Straight ahead

- Excusez-moi, pouvez-vous m'aider? (ehk-skoo-zay mwah, poo-vay voo mey-day) - Excuse me, can you help me?

Remember, practice makes perfect! Don't be shy to use these phrases and embrace the joy of communicating in French. Locals will appreciate your effort, and it can open doors to new experiences and connections.

And here's a friendly tip: keep a pocket-sized phrasebook or language app handy for quick reference on the go. It can be a real lifesaver when you need a little linguistic support.

So, my language-learning buddy, go forth and immerse yourself in the beautiful French language. From greetings to ordering a croissant, these basics will set you on the right path to navigate Brussels with confidence. Bonne chance (good luck), and have an amazing time exploring the city en français!

Safety and Security Advice

Safety and security should always come first when traveling. While Brussels is generally a safe city for tourists, it's important to stay vigilant and take necessary precautions to ensure a smooth and secure trip. Here are some friendly safety and security advice for your visit to Brussels:

1. Stay Aware of Your Surroundings: As with any destination, it's important to stay aware of your surroundings. Pay attention to your belongings and avoid displaying valuable items openly. Be cautious in crowded areas, public transportation, and tourist hotspots where pickpocketing can occur.

2. Keep Your Belongings Secure: Use a secure bag or backpack and keep it close to your body, preferably with zippers facing towards you. Consider using a money belt or hidden pouch to keep your valuables, passports, and cash safe.

It's also a good idea to make electronic copies of your important documents and store them securely online.

3. Use Reliable Transportation: Opt for licensed taxis or reputable ride-hailing services when getting around the city. Avoid getting into unregistered or unlicensed taxis. If you're using public transportation, be cautious of your belongings and keep an eye on your surroundings.

4. Maintain Contact: Share your vacation plans and contact information with a trusted friend or family member. Keep your mobile phone charged and have emergency contact numbers saved. It's also a good idea to have a local map or use GPS navigation to ensure you're on the right track.

5. Be Mindful of Scams: Like in any popular tourist destination, scams can occur. Be cautious of anyone offering unsolicited help or trying to distract you. Avoid street vendors selling counterfeit goods or suspicious deals that seem too good to be true. Trust your instincts and if something feels off, it's best to walk away.

6. Respect Local Laws and Customs: Familiarize yourself with the local laws and customs of Brussels. Dress modestly when visiting religious sites and be respectful of cultural practices. It's also important to know the emergency numbers of the country you're visiting.

7. Seek Advice from Local Authorities: If you have any concerns or need assistance, don't hesitate to seek help from local authorities, such as the police or tourist information centers. They can provide you with the most accurate and up-to-date information.

Remember, staying safe while traveling is about being aware, prepared, and taking common-sense precautions. By following these safety and security tips, you can have a worry-free and enjoyable trip to Brussels. Safe travels, and may your adventure be filled with wonderful memories!

Brussel Local Laws and Customs

When traveling to a new destination like Brussels, it's important to familiarize yourself with the local laws and customs to ensure a respectful and enjoyable experience. Here are some key local laws and customs to keep in mind:

Smoking Regulations: Belgium has strict smoking regulations. Smoking is generally prohibited in indoor public spaces, including restaurants, bars, and public transportation. Be sure to observe designated smoking areas and respect the no-smoking signs.

Alcohol Consumption: The legal drinking age in Belgium is 18 years old. It is generally acceptable to consume alcohol in public spaces, but excessive public drunkenness and disorderly behavior are frowned upon. Remember to drink responsibly and be mindful of your surroundings.

Cannabis Laws: The possession and use of cannabis are illegal in Belgium, although the enforcement of this law may vary. It is advisable to refrain from any involvement with illegal drugs and respect local regulations.

Dress Code and Etiquette: While there is no strict dress code in Brussels, it is advisable to dress modestly when visiting religious sites or formal establishments. It's also important to maintain general etiquette, such as being polite, respecting personal space, and using appropriate greetings.

Photography and Privacy: When taking photographs, be mindful of people's privacy and ask for permission when photographing individuals, especially in close-up shots. Avoid taking photos of sensitive areas like government buildings or military installations, as it may be prohibited.

Tipping: Tipping is not obligatory in Brussels, as service charges are usually included in the bill. However, it is customary to round up the bill or leave a small tip for good service, especially in restaurants or for taxi drivers.

Respecting local laws and customs is essential for creating a positive impression and enjoying a harmonious experience in Brussels. By familiarizing yourself with these aspects, you'll demonstrate cultural sensitivity and enhance your interactions with locals. Enjoy your time in Brussels and embrace the opportunity to immerse yourself in the local culture!

What To Do In-case Of An Emergency

As a tourist in Brussels, it's important to be prepared for any unforeseen emergencies. While we hope you won't encounter any major issues, it's always better to be safe than sorry. Here's what you should do in case of an emergency in Brussels:

1. Stay Calm and Assess the Situation: In any emergency, it's crucial to remain calm and assess the situation. Take a moment to gather your thoughts and evaluate the severity of the emergency.

2. Contact the Local Authorities: If you're facing a life-threatening situation or witnessing a crime, immediately contact the local authorities by dialing the emergency number, which is **112** in Brussels. This number will connect you to the police, fire services, or medical assistance as needed.

3. Seek Assistance from Your Accommodation: If you're staying in a hotel, hostel, or rented accommodation, inform the staff about the emergency. They can provide guidance, make necessary calls, or offer assistance.

4. Locate Nearest Hospitals or Medical Centers: Familiarize yourself with the nearest hospitals or medical centers in Brussels. In case of a medical emergency, call an ambulance by dialing **112** or ask your accommodation provider to assist you.

5. Contact Your Embassy or Consulate: If you face a situation that requires assistance from your home country's authorities, such as loss of passport or legal issues, contact your embassy or consulate in Brussels. They can provide guidance and support.

6. Follow Safety Guidelines: Pay attention to any safety instructions provided by authorities or local security personnel during emergencies. It's important to prioritize your safety and follow their guidance.

7. Keep Important Documents Secure: Always keep your important travel documents, including your passport, copies of identification, and travel insurance details, in a safe and secure place. This will make it easier to access them in case of loss or emergency.

Emergencies can be stressful, but staying calm, seeking assistance from local authorities, and following proper procedures will help you navigate through challenging situations. It's always a good idea to have emergency contact numbers and relevant information readily available. Here's hoping that your visit to Brussels will be safe, secure, and filled with wonderful memories!

Packing Essentials

Hey friend, let's talk about packing essentials for different weather and climates. Whether you're heading to a tropical paradise, a snowy wonderland, or a city with ever-changing weather like Brussels, it's important to pack smart and be prepared for whatever Mother Nature throws at you. Here are some friendly tips to help you pack your bags like a pro:

Layering is Key: No matter the destination, layering is your best friend. Packing lightweight clothing items that you can easily layer allows you to adjust to changing temperatures and weather conditions. Think of versatile pieces like t-shirts, long-sleeve shirts, cardigans, and jackets that you can mix and match.

Weather-Appropriate Clothing: Consider the weather and climate of your destination. If you're heading to a sunny beach, pack lightweight, breathable clothing like shorts, dresses, and swimwear. If you're venturing into colder climates, pack warm sweaters, thermal layers, and a good-quality jacket to keep you cozy.

Comfortable Shoes: Whether you're exploring cobblestone streets, hiking through nature trails, or strolling city blocks, comfortable shoes are a must. Pack a pair of sturdy walking shoes or sneakers that you can wear for long periods without discomfort. Don't forget to throw in some flip-flops or sandals for beach days or casual outings.

Weather-Proof Accessories: Be prepared for any weather surprises by packing weather-proof accessories. Bring a compact umbrella or a lightweight raincoat to stay dry during unexpected showers. A hat, sunglasses, and sunscreen are also essential for protection against the sun's rays.

Essentials for Every Climate: Regardless of the destination, there are a few essentials you should always have on hand. These include a versatile travel adapter, a small first-aid kit, a reusable water bottle, travel-size toiletries, and any necessary medications.

Research Your Destination: Before packing, do a little research on the weather patterns of your destination during your travel dates. Check the forecast, average temperatures, and any local weather phenomena that might affect your packing choices.

Remember, packing light and smart allows you more flexibility and ease during your travels. Stick to essentials, choose versatile pieces, and don't forget to leave some space in your luggage for souvenirs!

Happy travels, and may your adventures be filled with sunny skies and amazing experiences!

Tips for a Smooth Trip

Let's delve into some handy tips and tricks to ensure your journey is as smooth as silk. We want to help you navigate the road to travel bliss, where hiccups and hassles become a thing of the past. So, fasten your seatbelt and get ready for a seamless travel experience!

Plan and Prepare: Before setting off on your grand adventure, take the time to plan and prepare. Research your destination, create an itinerary, and make sure you have all the necessary travel documents. Stay organized by keeping digital copies of important documents, such as your passport and reservations, on your phone or in the cloud. This way, you'll have everything at your fingertips, ready to conquer any unforeseen circumstances.

Pack Smartly: Packing can be a daunting task, but fear not! Pack light, pack smart. Make a checklist of essentials, versatile clothing, and travel-sized toiletries. Roll your garments instead of folding them to conserve space and avoid creases. Don't forget a travel adapter, a portable charger, and a good book or playlist to keep you entertained during the journey. Packing like a pro ensures less stress and more freedom to explore.

Stay Informed: Stay up-to-date with travel advisories, weather forecasts, and any potential changes or disruptions that might affect your trip. Sign up for travel alerts from your airline or transportation providers to receive real-time updates. Knowledge is power, my friend, and staying informed allows you to adapt quickly and make informed decisions along the way.

Embrace Technology: In this digital age, technology can be your best travel companion. Download useful travel apps such as maps, language translators, and transportation guides. Use ride-sharing services or public transportation apps to get around efficiently. Let your smartphone be your trusty sidekick, providing information, and recommendations, and even helping you capture those picture-perfect moments.

Pack Snacks and Stay Hydrated: Hunger and dehydration can put a damper on your travel spirit. Pack some healthy snacks like granola bars or dried fruits to keep your energy levels up. Stay hydrated by carrying a refillable water bottle and refilling it whenever you have the chance. Small acts of self-care go a long way in keeping you happy and ready for adventure.

Be Flexible and Open-Minded: Travel is an ever-changing journey, my friend. Embrace flexibility and approach each new experience with an open mind. Unexpected delays or detours may lead to unexpected discoveries and serendipitous moments. So, let go of rigid expectations, savor the spontaneity, and allow yourself to be swept away by the magic of the unknown.

Connect with the Locals: Engage with the locals, my fellow explorer! Strike up conversations, ask for recommendations, and embrace cultural exchange. Locals often have invaluable insights, hidden gems, and insider tips that can take your trip to the next level. So, be open to making new connections and building bridges that transcend language and cultural barriers.

With these tips in your travel arsenal, you're ready to embark on a smooth and unforgettable journey. Remember, travel is not just about the destination—it's about the experiences, the connections, and the memories you create along the way. So, go forth, embrace the adventure, and may your travels be as smooth as a gentle breeze. Safe travels, my friend!

RECOMMENDED ITINERARY

7-Day Budget Traveler Itinerary

Day 1: Arrival and City Tour

- Morning: Arrive in Brussels and check into your budget-friendly accommodation. Take a leisurely stroll through the city center, starting with the magnificent Grand Place. Marvel at the stunning architecture and snap some Instagram-worthy photos.

- Afternoon: Visit the Royal Museums of Fine Arts of Belgium, taking advantage of discounted admission rates or free entry on certain days. Immerse yourself in the world of art and appreciate masterpieces by renowned artists.

- Evening: Explore the vibrant Saint-Géry area, where you'll find affordable bars and restaurants. Treat yourself to a local

Belgian beer or indulge in a tasty dinner at a budget-friendly eatery.

Day 2: Hidden Gems and Local Delights

- Morning: Discover the lesser-known neighborhood of Ixelles. Stroll through the vibrant streets, admiring the colorful street art and browsing the thrift shops for unique finds.

- Afternoon: Pay a visit to the Horta Museum, which is dedicated to the well-known Belgian architect Victor Horta. Marvel at the Art Nouveau designs and gained insight into his influential work.

- Evening: Grab a delicious and affordable meal at a local brasserie or sample street food at the lively Place Flagey. Don't forget to try a cone of freshly made frites to satisfy your cravings.

Day 3: Day Trip to Ghent and Bruges

- Morning: Take a day trip to Ghent, known for its medieval architecture and vibrant atmosphere. Explore the city center, visit the stunning Saint Bavo's Cathedral, and enjoy a picnic in the picturesque Graslei area.

- Afternoon: Continue your day trip to Bruges, a charming town straight out of a fairy tale. Wander through its cobblestone streets, visit the Markt square, and indulge in a sample of delicious Belgian chocolate.

- Evening: Return to Brussels and unwind in one of the city's parks, such as Parc du Cinquantenaire or Bois de la Cambre. Enjoy a peaceful evening surrounded by nature.

Day 4: Free and Low-Cost Activities

- Morning: Join a free walking tour of Brussels to discover the city's hidden gems and get insider tips from local guides. Don't forget to tip your guide as a token of appreciation.

- Afternoon: Visit the European Parliament area, where you can explore the Parliamentarium for free and learn about the history and functioning of the European Union.

- Evening: Grab dinner at one of the city's affordable food markets, such as Foodmet or the Place Sainte-Catherine market. Feast on a variety of cuisines at reasonable prices.

Day 5: Cultural Immersion

- Morning: Visit the Magritte Museum, dedicated to the renowned Belgian surrealist artist René Magritte. Delve into his fascinating world of art and uncover the secrets behind his thought-provoking creations.

- Afternoon: Explore the charming Sablon neighborhood, known for its antique shops and artisan boutiques. Browse for unique souvenirs and enjoy the ambiance of this picturesque district.

- Evening: Attend a free or low-cost cultural event, such as a music concert or art exhibition. Check local listings or seek advice from locals.

Day 6: Nature and Parks

- Morning: Take a trip to the Sonian Forest, a tranquil oasis just outside Brussels. Enjoy a peaceful hike or bike ride amidst lush greenery and connect with nature.

- Afternoon: Visit the Mini-Europe park, where you can marvel at miniature replicas of famous European landmarks. It's a budget-friendly way to travel the continent in just a few hours.

- Evening: Enjoy a picnic in one of Brussels' beautiful parks, such as Parc de Bruxelles or Parc Léopold. Relax, unwind, and soak up the tranquil atmosphere.

Day 7: Farewell Brussels

- Morning: Explore the vibrant Matonge district, known for its African influences and multicultural ambiance. Browse the colorful markets, try exotic flavors, and immerse yourself in the diverse cultural tapestry.

- Afternoon: Take a final walk through the charming streets of Brussels, making sure to savor one last cone of delicious Belgian waffles.

- Evening: Bid farewell to Brussels with a memorable dinner at a budget-friendly restaurant, toasting to the unforgettable experiences and new friendships forged during your budget travel adventure.

With this seven-day itinerary, you'll uncover the true essence of Brussels while keeping your wallet happy. Embrace the city's affordable delights, venture off the beaten path, and immerse yourself in the rich cultural tapestry that Brussels has to offer.

Throughout your journey, embrace the freedom of travel, interact with locals and fellow travelers, and allow yourself to be swept away by the captivating charm of Brussels. Let each step reveal new wonders and create unforgettable moments. Safe travels, adventurers, and may Brussels leave an indelible mark on your backpacking soul.

CONCLUSION

Well, my friend, we've reached the end of our Brussels budget travel guide! I hope you've found this book informative, entertaining, and above all, helpful for planning your budget-friendly adventure in this incredible city. As we wrap things up, I want to leave you with a big smile on your face and a few final words of wisdom.

Remember, traveling on a budget doesn't mean missing out on the best experiences. In fact, it often leads to the most memorable and unexpected moments. Embrace the thrill of finding hidden gems, exploring charming neighborhoods, and indulging in mouthwatering Belgian cuisine without breaking the bank.

Brussels has so much to offer, from the stunning architecture of Grand Place to the picturesque canals of Bruges, and the vibrant atmosphere of local festivals. Soak up the history, indulge in delicious waffles and chocolate, and immerse yourself in the rich culture of this fascinating city.

And hey, don't forget to try some of the local beer too! Belgium is famous for its brews, and what better way to relax and celebrate your budget-friendly adventures than with a pint of delicious Belgian beer?

Now, go forth and explore Brussels like a savvy traveler on a mission to create unforgettable memories. Remember to embrace the unexpected, keep an open mind, and be ready to laugh and share stories with fellow travelers along the way.

Thank you for joining me on this journey. I wish you an amazing time in Brussels, filled with joy, laughter, and unforgettable experiences. Safe travels, my friend, and may your budget be as happy as your heart is full! Cheers!

Printed in Great Britain
by Amazon

27300187R00088